IS THE INJEEL
CORRUPTED?

MY SEARCH FOR THE TRUTH
ABOUT THE NEW TESTAMENT

D0745799

BY FOUAD MASRI

IS THE INJEEL CORRUPTED?

©2006 by Fouad Masri

ISBN: 978-1-938512-15-5

Layout design by Wesleyan Publishing House.

Cover art by Alesa Bahler/Legacy Design.

Production design by Niddy Griddy Design, Inc.

Scripture quotations taken from The Holy Bible, New International Version® NIV® Copyright ©1973, 1978, 1984, 2011 by Biblica, Inc.TM Used by permission. All rights reserved worldwide.

Quotations from the Qur'an are taken from The Qur'an Translation, 27th US Edition, by Abdullah Yusuf Ali (Elmhurst, NY: Tahrike Tarsile Qur'an, Inc., 2011).

Printed in the United States of America

1 2 3 4 5 6 7 8 Printing/Year 17 16 15 14 13

DEDICATION

To all who love truth and are
willing to spread it

Dear Reader,

Praise God! Al Hamdulilah!

God gave me the strength to write this book, and I entrust to you my research on the Holy Injeel, the book given to Isa Al-Masih (Jesus the Christ), the son of Mary.

God sent Al-Injeel to enlighten us to His will and commands so that we can live a life of faith.

A life of faith in God (subhanahu wa ta'ala) is the greatest life someone could live. Faith is the fuel for meaning and success here on earth.

For this reason I offer this book to our Ummah. May it be a blessing to our needy world.

Abd Allah (the servant of God),

Fouad Masri

CHAPTER 1

المقدمة

INTRODUCTION

"The Injeel is corrupted." You've heard it. Maybe you have even said it.

When I was growing up in the Middle East, it was common for my professors and fellow classmates to dismiss the Injeel. They said Christians have changed it, and over the years it has lost its real meaning.

In high school my friend Kamal told me I shouldn't read the Injeel since it was unreliable and had been changed by Christians.

"Have you read the Injeel?" I asked Kamal.

"No."

"Then how do you know it's corrupted?" I reasoned. "You haven't
read it!"

"My grandfather and my uncle said
so," he replied.

I probed further, only to find that his
relatives who claimed the Injeel was
corrupted had never read the book
either.

> *This ... led me to
> investigate why the
> Injeel was disregarded,
> concealed, and treated
> as taboo by my
> teachers and peers.*

This exchange and others led me to investigate why the
Injeel was disregarded, concealed, and treated as taboo by
my teachers and peers.

To my surprise I found the Injeel is required for Muslims
to read and believe in. It is also required for Christians to
share. While my friends were treating the Injeel like bad
news, I found that Christians consider the Injeel good news.

THE MESSAGE OF GOD

Injeel is the Arabic word used for the Book of Prophet Jesus.
Εωανγγελιον (*Evangelion*), the book's original Greek title,
means good news. In Arabic the book was titled Injeel, and
Arab Christians in pre-Islamic times used this word to refer
to the New Testament, or the new covenant given by Christ.

The Injeel is the message of God for those who follow Jesus the Christ. The Injeel regulates every aspect of a Christian's life and beliefs.

Imams commonly teach that the Injeel is one of the four holy books Muslims are required to believe in, follow, and obey. If that is true, why is the Injeel not available in religious bookstores in many Muslim countries? If Muslims are to believe in the Injeel, why do some Islamic governments forbid their citizens to read it?

Is the Injeel really corrupted, as Kamal's uncle said it was? I wondered.

Muslims are obligated to honor Al-Qur'an Al-Karim and all of the holy books that God sent to humans: Al-Tawrat (the Book of Moses), Az-Zabur (the Book of David), and Al-Injeel (the Book of Jesus).

One man told me, "Muslims must honor these four books, but we follow only the Holy Qur'an" (Al-Qur'an Al-Karim). Therefore, the Injeel is not available in Muslim countries because many political and religious leaders believe the Injeel is corrupted. They follow the doctrine of tahrif, an idea that says Jews and Christians corrupted the original texts of the Tawrat and Injeel.

The common explanation is:

1.   Al-Tawrat (the Book of Moses) was corrupted,
        so God sent Az-Zabur (the Psalms of David).
2.   When Az-Zabur was corrupted, God sent
        Al-Injeel.
3.   Finally, when Al-Injeel was corrupted,
        God sent Al-Qur'an Karim.
4.   The Qur'an is incorruptible, for it is the word
        of God.

This illogical discourse stirred me to find out what it is about the Injeel that we are forbidden to know. Is the Injeel really corrupted? Did Christians change the Injeel?

I decided to study the Injeel and uncover its corruption for myself. I reasoned, *Why depend on the traditions of my community without investigating the facts? Most have never read the Injeel, yet they make judgments about its value. After all, many claimed the earth was flat until they studied the facts and found the earth is shaped as a sphere. Things are not always as they appear.*

The following is a summary of my research, which focused on answering a crucial question for those who submit to God: Is the Injeel corrupted?

CHAPTER 2

شهادة القرآن الكريم
THE QUR'ANIC WITNESS

WHAT DOES THE QUR'AN SAY ABOUT THE INJEEL?

To begin, I wanted to learn what the Qur'an says about this good news, or Injeel. In the Qur'an (Al-Qur'an Al-Karim) the Injeel is also referred to as the Book of Jesus.

Al-Injeel Is Sent from God

"Allah! there is no god but He the Living the Self-Subsisting Eternal. It is He Who sent down to thee (step by step), in truth, the Book confirming what went before it; and He sent down the Law (Of Moses) and the Gospel (of Jesus) before this as a guide to mankind and He sent down the Criterion (of judgment between right and wrong)" (Qur'an 3:2-4).

Muslims Must Read and Believe in the Injeel

*"Say ye: 'We believe in Allah and the revelation given
to us and to Abraham, Isma'il, Isaac, Jacob, and the
Tribes and that given to Moses and Jesus and that given
to (all) Prophets from their Lord we make no difference
between one and another of them and we bow to Allah
(in Islam)' " (Qur'an 2:136).*

*"Then in their wake We followed them up with (others
of) Our apostles: We sent after them Jesus the son
of Mary and bestowed on him the Gospel; and We
ordained in the hearts of those who followed him
Compassion and Mercy" (Qur'an 57:27).*

Christians Are Friends to Muslims

*"Nearest among them in love to the believers wilt thou
find those who say: "We are Christians": because
amongst these are men devoted to learning and men
who have renounced the world, and they are not
arrogant" (Qur'an 5:82).*

Christians Must Judge All Revelation by the Injeel

> *"Let the people of the Gospel Judge by what Allah hath revealed therein" (Qur'an 5:47).*

> *"Say: 'O People of the Book! Ye have no ground to stand upon unless ye stand fast by the Law, the Gospel, and all the revelation that has come to you from your Lord' " (Qur'an 5:68).*

God Keeps His Word

> *"Allah hath power over all things" (Qur'an 2:148).*

To my surprise I learned that many imams are teaching what is contrary to the previous Qur'anic verses. They say Al-Tawrat was corrupted, so God sent Az-Zabur. When Az-Zabur was corrupted, God sent Al-Injeel. Finally, the Injeel was corrupted so God sent the Qur'an. The Qur'an is incorruptible, for it is the word of God.

> *To my surprise I learned that many imams are teaching what is contrary to the Qur'an.*

However, the Qur'an, the holy book of Islam, never makes such a claim.

CHAPTER 3

صدق الله العظيم
LET GOD BE TRUE

WHAT DOES THE INJEEL
SAY ABOUT ITSELF?

The Qur'an seemed to point toward the credibility of the Injeel, but it seemed necessary to investigate the claims of the Injeel about itself. Listen to God's admonition and warning to Jews, Christians, and all humankind from the Injeel:

God Inspired All Scripture
> "All Scripture is inspired by God and is profitable for teaching, for rebuking, for correcting, for training in righteousness, so that the man of God may be complete, equipped for every good work" (2 Timothy 3:16-17).

"No prophecy of Scripture comes from one's own interpretation, because no prophecy ever came by the will of man; instead, men spoke from God as they were moved by the Holy Spirit" (2 Peter 1:20-21).

God's Words Stand Firm and Will Be Fulfilled

"Don't assume that I came to destroy the Law or the Prophets. I did not come to destroy but to fulfill. For I assure you: Until heaven and earth pass away, not the smallest letter or one stroke of a letter will pass from the law until all things are accomplished"
(Matthew 5:17-18).

"Heaven and earth will pass away, but My words will never pass away" (Matthew 24:35).

The Word of God Endures and Brings Life

"You have been born again—not of perishable seed but of imperishable—through the living and enduring word of God" (1 Peter 1:23).

God Protects His Word

"I testify to everyone who hears the prophetic words of this book: If anyone adds to them, God will add to him the plagues that are written in this book. And if anyone takes away from the words of this prophetic book, God will take away his share of the tree of life and the holy city" (Revelation 22:18-19).

Not only does the Injeel insist that God protects His Word, but the Zabur and Tawrat make this claim as well.

From the Tawrat

" 'As for Me, this is My covenant with them,' says the LORD: 'My Spirit who is on you, and My words that I have put in your mouth, will not depart from your mouth, or from the mouth of your children, or from the mouth of your children's children, from now on and forever,' says the LORD" (Isaiah 59:21).

From the Zabur

"LORD, Your word is forever; it is firmly fixed in heaven" (Psalm 119:89).

"Long ago I learned from Your decrees that You have established them forever" (Psalm 119:152).

"The entirety of Your word is truth, and all Your righteous judgments endure forever" (Psalm 119:160).

These verses stirred me. Christians would not dare alter or allow any change in their Holy Book, the Bible. Their respect for God and esteem for His commands are too great.

In fact, Christians would rather die than disobey and alter the Word of God.

After the resurrection of Jesus, His followers went from place to place proclaiming Christ as the Redeemer of the human race. Jewish leadership refused their words, and Roman and pagan emperors ridiculed what Jesus' followers said.

For Christianity's first three hundred years its followers were massacred, attacked, and tortured because of their faith, yet they refused to relent. As peaceful and pious people, they were unjustly abused for believing in Christ as the Savior of the universe. In many cases these martyrs of the Christian faith paved the way for the conversion of their persecutors.

The first Christians believed God's Word was true; they believed the previous verses show God as the powerful Creator of the universe who promised to keep and protect the Injeel.

CHAPTER 4

و لا غالب الا الله

NO ONE IS
STRONGER THAN
GOD ALMIGHTY

A THEOLOGICAL INVESTIGATION

As a mu'min (believer in God), I could not reconcile how God's Word could be changed by mere humans. *If God revealed the Injeel, I reasoned, wasn't it His responsibility to keep it from corruption?* We know God is the Creator of the universe: the sun, stars, and moon—everything we see. He created humans, their minds, and their intellects. God sees the hearts and knows the inner thoughts of sheikhs and citizens, businessmen and shepherds, scientists and artists. His knowledge spans time zones and time periods. He knows the past, present, and future. God knows everything!

ARE HUMANS STRONGER THAN GOD?

If God's Word was revealed to humans, and humans corrupted God's Word, doesn't that make humans stronger than God? Impossible!

Once I assume it is possible for God's Word and message to be corrupted, then *mere humans* like me become the measure of all things and not God Almighty (subhanahu wa ta'ala).

God sent the Injeel to enlighten people to the truth, and Jesus said the truth would set us free. Certainly humans are not stronger than the God who created them! No, they cannot corrupt the Injeel since it is God's Word.

WHAT PROPHET JESUS BELIEVED ABOUT GOD'S WORD

Jesus the Christ is the beloved Prophet of God (Habib Allah). He was chosen before birth (Mustafa Allah) to become the Redeemer (Al-Fadi) of the universe.

In the Injeel Prophet Jesus makes a promise in Bisharat Marcus, chapter 13, Aya 31: "Heaven and earth will pass away, but My words will never pass away."

The Injeel also says in 2 Timothy 3:16, "All Scripture is inspired by God." He authored it, and it belongs to Him.

The Injeel is clear about its origin: "First of all, you should know this: No prophecy of Scripture comes from one's own interpretation, because no prophecy ever came by the will of man; instead, men spoke from God as they were moved by the Holy Spirit" (2 Peter 1:20-21).

FAITH IN GOD, DOUBT IN MAN

My faith in a mighty God made me doubt those religious teachers who claimed the Injeel was corrupted. Astagh'furallah! May God forbid that His Word could ever be tarnished by mere men.

> *Astagh'furallah! May God forbid that His Word could ever by tarnished by mere men.*

Every time they accused the Injeel of being corrupted, they were blaspheming God. God sent the Injeel and has power over all things; He will preserve the Injeel as a testimony to all humans.

God is fair; He has protected His Word so that His verdict will be just when He judges each human by his or her response to the message of the Injeel.

No one can tamper with it. God has promised to keep it. And no one is stronger than God Almighty.

CHAPTER 5

ظهر الحق و زهق الباطل
ILLUSION VERSUS REALITY

A LOGICAL INVESTIGATION

Truth clearly stands out against error! God has given us the ability to seek truth, using not only our respect for God and His promises as a basis for belief but also logic and reasoning.

Humans are unique from all other creation in the way we gather information, process it, make conclusions about it, and finally transmit it to others. Our reasoning abilities are not threats to the truth; instead, they confirm it. If God created within me a mind that could reason, God would use this logic to support His own word and claims.

With this in mind, I set out to examine the corruption of the Injeel from a logical standpoint. Maybe God was not as powerful as I thought (Astagh'furallah).

The following pivotal questions and my deductive answers are the results of my search. In advance forgive my ignorance in doubting the power of God to keep His Word, the Injeel.

SEVEN PIVOTAL QUESTIONS

1. Who changed the Injeel?

For the Injeel to be changed, there needs to be a person or persons in history responsible for plotting and carrying out this scheme.

Who is the person who centered his or her efforts on changing a message sent from God? What evil person would corrupt the Injeel, betraying God and Christians?

Was the corruption performed by a Christian who believed in God's justice and Christ as the Redeemer? Or could a pagan or Jewish zealot have done this deed?

If such an infidel existed, history must reveal the person who deleted some information or added to the text of the Injeel in the years following the life of Christ.

2. Why was the Injeel changed?
Why would such a person corrupt the Injeel? If the Injeel contained enlightenment about the existence of God and God's beautiful plan for the world, what would motivate someone to change that revelation?

If the Injeel was changed, why would God allow early Christians to live in ignorance of God's will for nearly six hundred years (the time between the Injeel's supposed corruption and the coming of the prophet of Islam)? People are in a continual quest to know God's will. Why destroy that sought-after treasure for many generations?

If the Injeel contained enlightenment about the existence of God and God's beautiful plan for the world, what would motivate someone to change that revelation?

3. Where was the Injeel changed?
In what city or at what location was the Injeel corrupted? Did the discrepancy take place in a religious center or a political center? Which governments considered the Injeel a threat to them?

Rome, Byzantium, Alexandria, and Jerusalem—all of these were powerful epicenters of religious thought. But would any be more powerful than God Almighty? Can we find the original Injeel in that location and compare it to the present Injeel?

4. When was the Injeel changed?

At what point in history was the Injeel corrupted? According to Christian tradition, Jesus' death and resurrection occurred when Christ was in his 30s, making the event no earlier than A.D. 29 and no later than A.D. 33.

As we've already discussed, for three centuries after the life of Christ, Christians were persecuted and harshly oppressed. This leads us to a key question.

5. Did the Injeel's corruption take place *before* the coming of Prophet Muhammad or after?

Since the Prophet Muhammad commanded all Muslims to read the Injeel, it must have been corrupted after his death. He wouldn't have instructed us to believe and read a corrupted book, would he?

On the other hand, if the Injeel was corrupted before his time—or during his life—he surely would have mentioned it. If the Injeel has been corrupted since then, we need to go back in history and discover when.

6. Which parts were changed?

Many imams claimed corruption has found its way into the Injeel, but few would tell me which specific parts were affected.

Was the corruption thorough in that it affected the entire revelation of the Injeel? If so, is there any benefit to reading the message of the Injeel? If all of it is corrupted, why does the Qur'an require believing in it and reading it?

Perhaps only portions of the Injeel were changed. If only parts are corrupted, how can I discern truth from error? Was God able to protect some parts and not others?

7. Where is the original text?
This was a key question for me. All monotheistic religions affirm the coming of Jesus of Nazareth. So where is the true Injeel? As one devoted to God, I am required to study and respect the Injeel in obedience to God's commands. But how can I obey God by reading the Injeel if the original Injeel is lost? Would God allow such a mishap?

Because God sent Jesus and the Injeel to enlighten people for all generations, I must read the original text to fulfill my religious obligation.

THE FINAL REVELATION

One argument I heard was particularly intriguing. Some Muslim scholars pointed to the fact that since Islam came last chronologically, it had corrected the Injeel's errors and wrong ideas about God.

The Qur'anic verse most popularly used to support this idea was Qur'an 16:101-102:

> *"When We put a revelation in place of (another)*
> *revelation—and Allah knoweth best what He revealeth—*
> *they say: Lo! Thou art but inventing. Most of them*
> *know not.*

> *"Say: The holy Spirit hath delivered it from thy Lord*
> *with truth, that it may confirm (the faith of) those who*
> *believe, and as guidance and good tidings for those who*
> *have surrendered (to Allah)."*

Although the message of the Qur'an came last chronologically, its theological message is from the days of Prophet Abraham (Ibrahim), who called pagans to worship the one true God.

By the time the Qur'an was given to Muhammad, worshipers of one God had been guided for centuries by God's Word to Moses (Al-Tawrat), David (Az-Zabur), and Jesus (Al-Injeel).

Prophet Abraham (Ibrahim) was the first to submit himself to the one true God and turn away from his family's idolatrous past. He led his family from a pagan land to the place God led him.

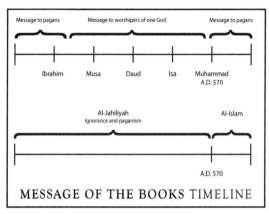

Figure 1. Although the message of the Qur'an came last chronologically, its theological message is from the days of Abraham.

MESSAGE OF THE BOOKS TIMELINE

The messages given to Moses (Musa), David (Daud), and Jesus (Isa) were primarily intended for a different audience altogether—the worshipers of one God. Therefore, God's revelation in the Tawrat, Zabur, and Injeel builds on the message of monotheism, carrying with it more advanced theological concepts, a greater understanding of God, and practical guidelines for living.

The culmination of God's revelation came through Prophet Jesus (Isa bin Maryam), the Word of God incarnate. His message was for all people, regardless of nationality, race, or language.

> *"Go, therefore, and make disciples of all nations,*
> *baptizing them in the name of the Father and of the*
> *Son and of the Holy Spirit, teaching them to observe*

everything I have commanded you. And remember, I am
with you always, to the end of the age"
(Matthew 28:19-20).

"I tell you that many will come from east and west,
and recline at the table with Abraham, Isaac, and
Jacob in the kingdom of heaven" (Matthew 8:11).

"There is no Jew or Greek, slave or free, male or female;
for you are all one in Christ Jesus" (Galatians 3:28).

The Qur'an never presumes to replace the earlier messages from God.

The Qur'an, on the other hand, came to Arabs who were worshiping many gods and denied monotheism. This was Al-Jahiliyah, or the time of ignorance. It came as a wake-up call to the people of the Arabian Peninsula. Thus, the Qur'an's assertion that the message was in Arabic, to be understood by Arab tribes:

"We have made it a Qur'an in Arabic, that ye may be
able to understand" (Az-Zukhruf 43:3).

In addition, the Qur'an repeatedly highlights that its message confirms what came before; it never presumes to replace the earlier messages.

> *"To thee We sent the Scripture in truth, confirming the scripture that came before it, and guarding it in safety: so judge between them by what Allah hath revealed"* (Al-Ma'idah 5:48).

CHANGING THE WORDS OF GOD

Some Muslims cite the following verses in the Qur'an as evidence that Christians have changed the words of God.

> *"Those unto whom We gave the Scripture recognize (this revelation) as they recognize their sons. But lo! a party of them knowingly conceal the truth"* (Al-Baqara 2:146).

> *"O followers of earlier revelation! Why do you cloak the truth with falsehood and conceal the truth of which you are [so well] aware?"* (Al-Imran 3:71).

> *"Those who conceal the clear (Signs) We have sent down, and the Guidance, after We have made it clear for the people in the Book, 'on them shall be Allah's curse, and the curse of those entitled to curse' "* (Al-Baqara 2:159).

The previous verses do not refer to people who changed the words of God but those who concealed it. God is stronger than any human, and while humans may try to conceal God's Word, His truth still clearly stands out from error.

FEAR OF TRUTH

In my search for answers to these questions, I was shocked by the ignorance of the religious leadership in my community. They seemed afraid of the questions; these ideas were not allowed to be discussed. I was accused of venturing where I should not go. *Why not read the Injeel?* I asked myself.

Some leaders tried to prove the corruption with dates, events, and places, but when I further investigated their claims, the only thing that became clear was their ignorance about the life of Prophet Jesus, the Injeel, and the Christian religion.

Friends of mine were hostile to my quest for truth. I was even harassed and questioned about my interest in reading and studying the New Testament.

Why the hostility? I was only looking for the Injeel so that I could become a good believer in God. Their logic was worse than their character. They were bloodthirsty instead of God-thirsty.

At this point my investigation led me to look at the historical evidence for the credibility of the Injeel and why Christians follow it.

CHAPTER 6

وأرسلنا الانجيل هدى للعالمين
THE MANUSCRIPTS SPEAK

A HISTORICAL INVESTIGATION

My search for answers led me to an extensive examination of the historical context and manuscripts of the Injeel.

I discovered that the Injeel is highly revered among Christians. They have taken great care to protect it from corruption. The history of the Injeel can be divided into three historical time periods:

A. Eyewitness stage
B. Persecution stage
C. Translation stage

A. EYEWITNESS STAGE (A.D. 0-100)

Prophet Jesus (pbuh) was born to the virgin Mary as a miracle from God. His birth was foretold by prophets like Isaiah.

Virgin Birth Foretold

> *"The Lord Himself will give you a sign: The virgin will conceive, have a son, and name him Immanuel"* (Isaiah 7:14).

City Foretold

> *"Bethlehem Ephrathah, you are small among the clans of Judah; One will come from you to be ruler over Israel for Me. His origin is from antiquity, from eternity"* (Micah 5:2).

In the previous verses you can see that the coming of Prophet Isa (Jesus, the son of Mary) was prophesied hundreds of years in advance. The Tawrat was clear that the Messiah would come to lead people to the truth of God's law.

Jesus, the son of Mary, was the promised Messiah of the Jews.

> *"He first found his own brother Simon and told him, 'We have found the Messiah!' (which means 'Anointed One')"* (John 1:41).

This same Jesus was sinless from birth and a leader of many believers. He raised the dead and healed the sick. His teachings and words were recorded in the book Al-Injeel.

Al-Injeel is Arabic for the Greek word *Evangelion*. Jesus and His followers spoke Koine Greek, the trade language under the Roman Empire. Scholars also agree that Jesus understood and spoke at least three languages: Koine Greek, Aramaic, and Hebrew.

Manuscripts

At present no one has found the original copies of any religious texts. We do not have the original, physical copy of Al-Qur'an Al-Karim, nor do we have Uthman's copy.

We also do not have the original, physical copy of the Tawrat, Zabur, or Injeel today. We have manuscripts that were hand copied and passed from one generation to another.

The scribes were serious about copying the Injeel because it was God's Word to enlighten humans. The Injeel warned them against tampering with the revelation of God in any way:

> *"I testify to everyone who hears the prophetic words of this book: If anyone adds to them, God will add to him the plagues that are written in this book. And if anyone*

takes away from the words of this prophetic book, God
will take away his share of the tree of life and the holy
city, written in this book" (Revelation 22:18-19).

EYEWITNESSES TO EVENTS IN THE INJEEL

While eyewitnesses to Jesus' birth, death, and resurrection
were still living, any misrepresentation of Jesus' teachings or
character would have been rejected. These people knew the
truth.

"Many have undertaken to compile a narrative about
the events that have been fulfilled among us, just as the
original eyewitnesses and servants of the word handed
them down to us. It also seemed good to me, since I
have carefully investigated everything from the very first,
to write to you in an orderly sequence" (Luke 1:1-3).

"We did not follow cleverly contrived myths when we
made known to you the power and coming of our Lord
Jesus Christ; instead, we were eyewitnesses of His
majesty" (2 Peter 1:16).

We know these eyewitnesses firmly testified to what they
had seen. What they wrote couldn't be disputed; everyone
else had witnessed the same events and would correct them
if they were wrong.

At the same time, if the followers of Christ incorrectly transcribed His words from the beginning, the Injeel and, subsequently, the Christian faith would never have existed.

To believe God sent the Injeel, we must first accept that God made sure it was recorded and copied correctly. Otherwise, people could not be judged by what was written in it. God's revelation must be perfect to ensure his righteous judgment.

In the eyewitness stage there was no opportunity for corrupting the Bible, because the eyewitnesses were alive. Those who were alive and knew the truth—whether believers or not—would protest any changes to the story.

For example, if I wrote a history book claiming John F. Kennedy was never assassinated or Martin Luther King Jr. never gave his famous "I have a dream" speech or that America's astronauts never walked on the moon, people would dismiss it as heresy; eyewitnesses to JFK's assassination, King's speech, and the U.S. moonwalk are still living. In 50 to 100 years people might consider buying my book. But as long as the eyewitnesses are alive, I cannot deny or re-create any major historical events.

The same is true for the major events in the Injeel. No one during the eyewitness stage could dispute a historical fact.

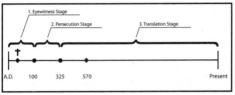

Figure 2. The three stages, spanning from Jesus' resurrection in 33 A.D. (C.E.) to the present are grouped to demonstrate the Injeel's trustworthiness throughout history.

In addition to these eyewitnesses being alive and attesting to the truth of the Injeel's message, two other facts—martyrdom and the proof of the resurrection—also contribute to the Injeel's trustworthiness:

1. No one will die for a lie they made up.

Usually people lie for personal gain or to cover an embarrassing situation. Many followers of Prophet Jesus died claiming that Jesus is the Messiah who died and rose again.

2. No conclusive evidence was available for Jesus' staying in the grave.

Eyewitnesses who were opposed to Christ could have brought the body of Jesus to Christians as proof that denies the resurrection. If they could have, they would have!

Such is the case with the Injeel in this stage. The eyewitness stage begins at the birth of Jesus and ends in the year A.D. 100. The last eyewitnesses to Jesus' life, death, and resurrection could not have survived after the year A.D. 100. The community of eyewitnesses—whether following Christ or not—would have died by A.D. 100.

After the last eyewitness died around A.D. 100, the first opportunity to change God's Word would arise. If an infidel wanted to corrupt God's Word, he now had his chance.

B. PERSECUTION STAGE (A.D. 100-325)

In this time period Christians everywhere were persecuted. Jewish leaders harassed and killed them. The Romans considered them atheists since they did not believe in a pantheon of gods. Considering Christians a great threat, Romans ordered them killed and burned along with their books.

In this age of persecution against Jesus' followers, it is highly unlikely that changes entered the Injeel. The four evidences proving the Injeel's integrity during this time period are:

1. Manuscripts
2. Lectionaries
3. Early translations
4. Church fathers

Let's take a deeper look at each piece of evidence.

1. Manuscripts
The books of the New Testament were copied by hand on manuscripts made of papyri. Papyrus is a plant that grows in Egypt. When Egyptians invented paper from papyri, different colors of ink were used to write in hieroglyphs.

A Brief History
The Phoenicians borrowed the Egyptian's invention and wrote using the alphabet, spreading the message to the known world from Byblos. The early Christians started copying the books of the Injeel as the manuscripts deteriorated and new churches were established. After the last surviving disciple, John, was exiled to the island of Patmos and later died, Christians copied the books of the Injeel with renewed passion, distributing them among the churches.

Most members of the Christian community couldn't afford a personal copy of the entire Injeel. Partial manuscripts—a few books of the New Testament, not the entire text—were therefore produced, distributed, and shared among Christian believers.

Another type of partial manuscript is the copies of the Injeel found in the ruins of Christian homes and churches. These are partial due to age or deterioration through time, not original copy.

Partial manuscripts dating from A.D. 100 to A.D. 325 include the whole books of the Injeel, accounts of the crucifixion and resurrection of Christ, and records of the uniqueness of Jesus and His atoning death.

2. Lectionaries

The existence of church lection-aries is one of the most important evidences of the New Testament's credibility, yet it is often the least studied, least known, and least used. Lection-aries contain the appointed readings (or "lections") for each day of the church year. As such, they were extremely important to individual churches.

Since many Christians did not own a personal copy of the Injeel, they depended on these service books for learning and growing in the knowledge of God's Word.

Figure 3. One famous papyrus fragment, P52, is dated from before 150 A.D. It contains a portion of the Book of John.

The number of known lectionaries has jumped to about 2,300 copies. In addition, almost 3,200 continuous-text manuscripts exist, bearing witness to the widespread and widely read nature of the Injeel during this time frame.

3. Early Translations

Complete manuscripts of the Injeel translated from Greek to other Mediterranean languages are important in verifying the New Testament's reliability. One such copy in Syriac is known as the Peshitto. Translations such as this can be reverse translated to check its reliability with the original Greek manuscripts.

4. Church Fathers

Leaders of the Christian community who were followers of Christ's disciples were known as church fathers.[1] You could call them second-generation disciples.

Following Christ under severe persecution, they led their communities to faith in Christ. While living in different areas around the Mediterranean Sea, they corresponded with one another through written letters and sermons. Their

---

1. A partial listing of church fathers:

Early Church

A.D. 301	Alexander, Bishop of Lycopolis
A.D. 260–311	Peter, Bishop of Alexandria

Apostolic Fathers

A.D. 30–100	Saint Clement
A.D. 130	Mathetes, "the Unknown Disciple"
A.D. 69–155	Polycarp
A.D. 30–107	Ignatius John Papias
A.D. 70–155	Justin Martyr
A.D. 110–165	Irenaeus

writings are still available today for study and comparison to the earliest complete manuscript (Codex Sinaiticus) in existence.

These letters and sermons have been uncovered around the Mediterranean Sea, with quotations and passages in total agreement with today's texts.

C. TRANSLATION STAGE
(A.D. 325-PRESENT)

The Injeel was faithfully copied and distributed as Christianity spread throughout Europe, Africa and Asia. As the Injeel was reproduced into different languages, translators were meticulous in keeping each copy consistent with the manuscripts.

Today, all translations in different languages are copied from early manuscripts. The most recognized are:

1. Codex Sinaiticus
2. Codex Vaticanus
3. Codex Alexandrinus

Versions
Some claim that the many different versions of the Injeel have corrupted its intended meaning. Version in English means translation. When famous Muslim debaters claim

that a version of the Bible means another version of the story, they are only exposing their ignorance of the English language.

Some who claim to be an authority on the Christian Bible are ignorant of basic Hebrew and Greek, the primary languages of the Bible. Just as it is absurd for a person untrained in Arabic to claim himself

Figure 4. Codex Sinaiticus, one of the most important manuscripts of the New Testament, was discovered in Egypt in 1859.

an authority on the Qur'an, it is just as important to learn the biblical languages (Hebrew and Koine Greek) to be an authority on the Bible.

History Is Speaking

What is history saying to us? A careful look at Christian history from the death and resurrection of Christ to the present day reveals a thread of faithfulness to the preservation of God's revealed Word.

From first-century eyewitness accounts (eyewitness stage) to quoted Scripture in letters sent among persecuted believers (persecution stage) to the early copies of God's Word available from as early as A.D. 325 (translation stage), the manuscripts are speaking to us. They are speaking the same consistent message of Jesus today that was lived and recorded nearly two thousand years ago.

A careful look at Christian history from the death and resurrection of Christ to the present day reveals a thread of faithfulness to the preservation of God's revealed Word.

"[Jesus] said, 'Anyone who has ears to hear should listen!' " (Mark 4:9).

CHAPTER 7

تعرفون الحق و الحق يحرركم
WHAT DOES
ALL THIS MEAN?

I n this study I have attempted to understand my friends'
and neighbors' unfounded claims that the Injeel is corrupted. What I found not only
convinced me the Injeel has
been preserved and kept by God
but also challenged me to believe
and stake my life on its message.

*The book we hold in our
hands today is the same
story believed by the early
followers of Jesus. They
lived and died by that firm
belief.*

Historically, the overwhelming
evidence available to us today
not only speaks; it shouts! The
evidence only verifies the truth
and pure nature of the Injeel.
The manuscripts and early textual proofs clearly point to
the truth about the Injeel. The book we hold in our hands

today is the same story believed by the early followers of Jesus. They lived and died by that firm belief.

Logically, we found that one must answer some pivotal questions before he accuses the Injeel of corruption, questions such as:

- When was the Injeel corrupted?
- Who would do such a thing?
- What motivation would someone have to change the Injeel?

Besides, it is unlikely that the closest adherents and followers of a religion—all twelve disciples—would die for their beliefs if they had been lying all along.

Many who claimed the Injeel was corrupted were simply misinformed about its origin and message. Their claims were not supported by any research or logical proof. Because of their ignorance they have led many away from the path of understanding. In an attempt to speak for God, they have failed to give Him the respect and admiration He deserves for protecting and keeping the Injeel!

Finally, in order to believe in a Creator with power over all things, a God who communicates with His creation and remains a just Judge based on what He has revealed, one must accept that God sent us His Word, Jesus. We must accept that the Injeel has been protected by God for the sake of humanity's enlightenment (lihuda al-alamiin).

God Almighty used this study to compel me to faith in God and the Redeemer, Jesus the Messiah. Today I invite you to enter the family of Jesus by making the following prayer. Christ can give you power to live in obedience to God.

Prayer is simply a conversation with God Almighty, done anywhere you are, at any time of day or night.

> *Almighty God, You are the merciful God. I repent of my sin and self-righteous attitude. I believe in You and Your Word, Jesus the Messiah. I commit to follow your teachings in the Injeel until my last breath.   Amen.*

APPENDIX 1

Terms

Allah—the Arabic name for God, meaning *the one God.*

Astagh'furallah—the Arabic word used by Christians and Muslims to entreat forgiveness in the event of blasphemous words or sinful behavior.

codex—a type of manuscript that consists of pages of papyri with writings on front and back. These are collected in a specific order and bound by leather or wood.

imam—the lay religious leader or professional cleric of a Muslim community or mosque; leads in Friday salat (noon congregational prayers).

Injeel—the Arabic name given to the Book of Jesus. It is mentioned in the Qur'an as the book revealed to Prophet Jesus and followed by Christians, the New Testament.

Isa—the Qur'anic and Arabic name for Jesus (English) or Yesua (Hebrew). In the Qur'an Jesus is called Kalimat Allah, "the Word of God," "the breath from God," and "a prophet of the Book." Muslims consider Jesus to be one of the five or six authentic prophets.

Isa al-Masih—Jesus the Messiah

manuscripts—earliest known writings of religious texts from which all subsequent translations are based.

Muhammad—praised; the chosen one, the prophet and founder of Islam, considered by Muslims to be khatem al-anbiya, the Seal (last) and greatest of the prophets. Born A.D. 570, died A.D. 632.

mu'min—believer; in contrast to an unbeliever, kafir.

Tawrat—the Qur'anic name given to the Torah of Moses.

ummah—community; a group bound by ancestry, religion, nation, race, occupation, or common cause.

Zabur—the Qur'anic name given to the Psalms of David.

APPENDIX 2

Nicene (or Nicaean) Council

The Nicene Council was an ecumenical or worldwide council that sought to unify the Christian church by addressing certain issues relating to the Christian faith. Although previous church councils had met throughout Christian history, the Council of Nicaea was important due to its sponsorship by the Emperor Constantine.

In A.D. 325 Constantine invited bishops and church leaders from the Mediterranean and beyond to the meeting held in Nicaea, Asia Minor, near what was then Constantinople.

Discussion centered on the religious texts read and taught in churches and their implications for the Christian faith. The leaders sought to answer this question: What, of these texts, is not the Word of God?

The criteria set resulted in what is known today as the New Covenant (to Arab Christians, the Injeel). Some texts that failed to meet the strict criteria were called Pseudo pigroipha (today Pseudepigrapha), or false writings.

Books categorized as Pseudepigrapha were written by individuals who were not contemporaries of Jesus or eyewitnesses to his life, death, and resurrection. Some of these writings can be found in what is known as *The Apocryphal New Testament*.

The Nicene Council developed criteria for what is not considered the Word of God. Many wrongfully accuse the Nicene Council for deciding what Scripture was the Word of God. Instead, the council simply affirmed what the church for centuries had considered inspired and developed criteria for determining errant texts.

APPENDIX 3

Carbon Dating of Manuscripts

Radiocarbon dating is a radiometric dating method that uses the naturally occurring isotope carbon-14 to determine the age of carbonaceous materials. In addition to binding, handwriting, and paper type, it is one of the methods commonly used to date ancient manuscripts.

Through the use of radiocarbon dating and other factors such as handwriting, historians generally agree on the dates for the three earliest manuscripts of the New Testament.

They are:

Codex Vaticanus (A.D. 300)—has resided in the Vatican since the Middle Ages and remains there today.

Codex Sinaiticus (A.D. 350)—on permanent display in the British Library along with other early biblical manuscripts.

Codex Alexandrinus (A.D. 450)—transferred from the Christian Library in Alexandria to the British Library in the 17th century, where it still resides today.

APPENDIX 4

Translations of the Bible

The Injeel was originally written in Koine Greek, the language of the common people in the Roman Empire. Scholars have taken great care to translate the Bible's message into many languages so that people from all nations and backgrounds can read and understand it.

Some people might accuse translators of changing the meaning of the New Testament. This is far from the truth. Committees of dedicated scholars ensure that every translation reflects the original Greek texts. Christians consider the Bible a holy Book, handling it with respect and honoring the original manuscript in every translation.

In the final analysis those who doubt the credibility of individual translations should consider studying Koine Greek in order to read the New Testament in its earliest form. When I did that, I found the study of the New Testament Greek manuscripts to be fruitful and intellectually—as well as spiritually—satisfying. I trust you will find it the same.

APPENDIX 5

The Five Pillars of Christianity:
What Every Christian Believes

Did you know Christians across the face of the earth are unified by five core beliefs? We call these the Five Pillars of Christianity.

1. One God—Christians believe in one God.

"Even if there are so-called gods, whether in heaven or on earth—as there are many 'gods' and many 'lords'—yet for us there is one God, the Father. All things are from Him, and we exist for Him" (1 Corinthians 8:5-6).

2. One Savior—Christians are redeemed by one Savior.

"[Grace] has now been made evident through the appearing of our Savior Christ Jesus, who has abolished death and has brought life" (2 Timothy 1:10).

3. One Spirit—Christians are filled and empowered by one Spirit.

"You will receive power when the Holy Spirit has come on you, and you will be My witnesses in Jerusalem, in all Judea and Samaria, and to the ends of the earth" (Acts 1:8).

4. One message—Christians are unified by one message.

> "Jesus went to Galilee, preaching the good news of God:
> 'The time is fulfilled, and the kingdom of God has come
> near. Repent and believe in the good news!' "
> (Mark 1:14-15).

5. One family—Christians are part of one family.

> "There is no Jew or Greek, slave or free, male or female;
> for you are all one in Christ Jesus." (Galatians 3:28).

APPENDIX 6

Five Practices of Christians Who Are Following Jesus

1. Obey the Commands of Christ

"Do not offer any part of yourself to sin as an instrument of wickedness, but rather offer yourselves to God as those who have been brought from death to life; and offer every part of yourself to him as an instrument of righteousness." (Romans 6:13)

"I am the true vine, and my Father is the gardener. He cuts off every branch in me that bears no fruit, while every branch that does bear fruit he prunes so that it will be even more fruitful. You are already clean because of the word I have spoken to you. Remain in me, and I will remain in you. No branch can bear fruit by itself; it must remain in the vine. Neither can you bear fruit unless you remain in me. I am the vine; you are the branches. If a man remains in me and I in him, he will bear much fruit; apart from me you can do nothing." (John 15:1-5)

2. Pray

"Rejoice always, pray continually, give thanks in all circumstances; for this is God's will for you in Christ Jesus." (1 Thessalonians 5:16-18)

"And when you pray, do not be like the hypocrites, for
they love to pray standing on the street corners to be seen
by men. I tell you the truth, they have received their
reward in full. But when you pray, go into your room,
close the door and pray to your Father, who is unseen.
Then your Father, who sees what is done in secret, will
reward you. And when you pray, do not keep on babbling
like the pagans, for they think they will be heard because
of their many words. Do not be like them, for your Father
knows what you need before you ask him."
(Matthew 6:5-8)

3. Study the Bible

"Continue in what you have learned and have become
convinced of, because who know those from whom you
learned it, and how from infancy you have known the
Holy Scriptures, which are able to make you wise for
salvation through faith in Christ Jesus. All Scripture
is God-breathed and is useful for teaching, rebuking,
correcting and training in righteousness, so that the
servant of God may be thoroughly equipped for every
good work." (2 Timothy 3:14b-17)

*"Do not merely listen to the word, and so deceive
yourselves. Do what it says. Anyone who listens to the
word but does not do what it says is like a man who
looks at his face in a mirror and, after looking at himself,
goes away and immediately forgets what he looks like.
But the man who looks intently into the perfect law that
gives freedom, and continues to do this, not forgetting
what he has heard, but doing it - he will be blessed in
what he does." (James 1:22-25)*

4. Have Fellowship with Other Believers

*"And let us consider how we may spur one another
on toward love and good deeds, not giving up meeting
together, as some are in the habit of doing, but
encouraging one another – and all the more as you see
the Day approaching." (Hebrews 10:24-25)*

5. Testify to Non-Believers

*"[Jesus] said to them, 'Go into all the world and preach
to gospel to all creation. Whoever believes and is baptized
will be saved, but whoever does not believe will be
condemned.' " (Mark 16:15-16)*

*"And whatever you do, whether in word or deed, do it all
in the name of the Lord Jesus, giving thanks to God the
Father through him." (Colossians 3:17)*

UNLOCK THE TRUTH

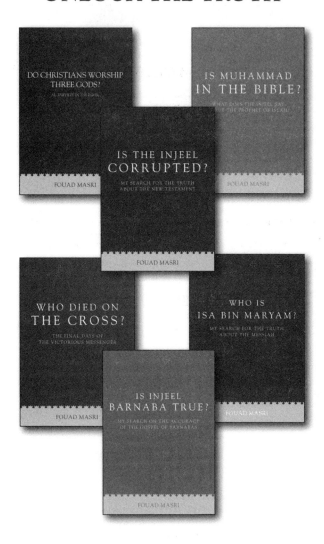

To order these resources, go to www.unlockthetruth.net.

HOW CAN I GET A COPY OF THE INJEEL?

IS THE INJEEL CORRUPTED?
RESPONSE FORM

☐ I would like a copy of the Injeel. Please send me one free of charge.

    Language preference:_____

☐ Send me an in-depth study on the teachings of Jesus.

☐ I would like to follow Jesus Christ as my Savior.

Name _____

Address _____

City _____

State_____ Zip Code _____

Country_____

Phone _____

Complete form and mail to:

Crescent Project
P.O. Box 50986
Indianapolis, IN 46250

Or via email:
info@crescentproject.org

During Eid Al-Adha, many Muslims sacrifice a
sheep or ram to commemorate the holy event when
God redeemed the son of Abraham.

BUT WHAT IS THE CHRISTIAN ADHA?

Learn from the Injeel why God required
sacrifice in the New Testament.

**Contact us to request a copy of
Adha in the Injeel (Arabic/English).**

To get more of these resources go to
unlockthetruth.net or fouadmasri.com.